Along the Fault of Me

Along the Fault of Me

Poems

Diane Corson

Salon Argyle Press
Portland, Oregon
2024

ISBN 979-8-3303614-5-8

dianencorson.wixsite.com

Cover design: Sage Corson
Cover art: Diane Corson

Interior: Diane Corson photographs—
Pollen Floating on Oil on Water

Salon Argyle
Portland, Oregon

With my heartfelt appreciation:

Bruce Parker: Editorial, Portland,
    Oregon

Lucy Cotter: Editorial, Portland, Oregon

B Sedgwick: Editorial, Portland, Oregon

With thanks for their lovely reflections:

Lucy Cotter: Portland, Oregon

Tristan Beach: Reno, Nevada

for my girls: Hallie, Effie, and Sage

If at length the smouldering anguish
Will not overcome —

        —Emily Dickinson

*There is nothing of me that is alone and
absolute except my mind, and we shall
find that the mind has no existence by
itself, it is only the glitter of the sun on
the surface of the waters.*

        —D. H. Lawrence

Contents

leaving you to be me
personae

How I Made It 3

How I Found Me 5

I Want Your Head 7

Disposed 9

I am of the Sea 11

empty emptiness 13

august nights 15

Before I Die 17

She Sat Beside Herself with a Note from
        Him 19

and mine 21

The Passing of Me 23

Pigeon's Morsel 25

the men I have not adored 27

just now i am me 31

profound state of unease
ecology

In Creation   35

Moonlit Leaves   37

chasing rabbits 39

The Cello Project   41

The Secret Life of Her   43

With His Breath   45

Clothes Lines   47

Narcissus   49

Lip It   51

sfumato of her lips
ekphrastic

Small Shadows   55

The Art of Distance   57

Paterson's Way   59

Alice and Me   63

Biutiful   65

My Own Cave   67

IN DUCTION 69

The Refusal of Time 71

entwined vines
love

I Have Loved You 77

where the spring sighs 79

My Alice 81

Entwined Vines 83

The Moon and You 85

edges 87

Flower Petals 89

His Hair Like Wings 91

my memories 93

Wings My Whisper 95

/Us in a Timezone 97

in memory: the air
nature/eco-nature

Elegy for a Douglas Fir 101

Coastal Range 103

Hummingbirds 105

Limb by Limb   107

The Spring   109

Sandy River   111

Andaman Sea   113

Nature Retreat   115

Light Beyond the Trees   117

ode to green   119

anguish that i held
emotion

anguish   123

Fog at the Door   125

The Seagull and the River   127

Moonlight as Snow   129

the poker and the fire   131

Wave   133

Existence   135

About the Author   138

About the Book   140

leaving you to be me

personae

How I Made It

was

how i made it
(actually, i didn't
come here by choice)
yes, i know what a beautiful place

was

an iceberg that stood
when polar bears dove freely
now without their skins
having been draped over others

was

i cannot guess
and it was not luck
maybe timing
anything i do not know about

was

where i stood with red shoes
red pants pantaloon style
head gone bald
body held up by debris
coke cans, airplanes
        oaken ships
cars driven by octopi, chests full of gold
        it has been said

filled with porcelain vases, gold
intentions, greed, crowbars, cadavers

was

intentional in our realm
when less the time
felt like nothing mattered
while everything does —

was

a spotted bunny in a truck
rolled thru streets
unidentified as they drove into the sea
at the head of a freighter

and the gray duck hums

How I Found Me

I remember you were always
                some distance
away, my eyes followed trails
        you left
                in the snow
once you left me a pink glove —
other times only broken windows —
In the snow your kisses — woke the bees
        melted snow made streams
your loosened hair
        cascaded and puddled
under the shouts of children
puddles were meant
        to teach me something —
my thoughts bled — into a confluence
        of hilltops
        where melting snow
        trickled less

your bay took my imagination everywhere
        *on **little** sailboats*
nameless winds wrapped promises
        around me
sleep looked hard to find me —
I recall a lamentation of onions and citrus
        a revelation from a wound, a knife
cut
        homemade tortillas
                the ritual of corn
        and the penance
of kneaded dough

I wanted to crawl
        under your fingernails
so I could remember what
        your hands had been like there

I Want Your Head
     After: Artemisia Gentileschi's painting
     —Judith Slaying Holofernes

I paint at night so as to not be seen
I paint at night by candle light
I shall not go back and sit behind my
          father
Being born in 1593 has been a bitch
I am a modern woman
I arrange my still life without you
          Bouquets of flowers, oysters
          pomegranates —
          dusty bottles of wine —
          do not appeal to me
I want women in action, women who slay
— to paint them not with the usual flesh
          of their doing
I have my name on my paintings
And I want your head

Disposed
  Kenton Park, Portland

It wasn't so much that she knew
what she was doing
no one had ever talked to her about
her future
what might become of her
she hadn't realized, by then it was too
late, until she had been entirely disposed

she tried being a vendor
a hawker in a park and gave away bits
          of   herself
to provoke and instigate
who would then like her
or were attracted to her
          mostly the curious —

when people — for now she would
call them friends — they walked away
with her

her flesh, her skin, with a nail
and once it was a leg —
an eyeball —
it made her
wink

they winked back   with
their three eyes
which scratched her DNA
to go on somewhere

she smiled at each person as bits
of her fled —
into their futures

Her flesh, her skin, *herself* — a future

I am of the Sea

There isn't much that doesn't remind me
of you
the wind, the waves of this sea
the coming into harbor
our old boat, the Fitzcarraldo, couldn't
have handled this

I swim along rather splendidly, after all
while everything reminds me of you
the trees on the hills
the grains of sand at the shore
the waves of the sea
the distance between our seas
is vast
grown by choice: yours then mine
now mine are firm
my sea
parts for me
I do not part for you
I remain ebbing and flowing: constant

After thirty years of a fractured life
together
there still is thought
while the pain ate away at me then
the denial of me then hangs now

Now I am of the sea
I linger on a ship
crossing the San Juan Channel

then with ease through the Upright
Channel
on board the Electra Number 2E
I have a name

It is I. I am. I am me

Then the Guemes Channel to Anacortes
          —Washington
then home to my own
bring me home
I am with the sea

empty emptiness

as i look at trees
i realize they will be the last ones
standing
who withstand

unexpected measures of emptiness

the first tree (one) goes like this
— — —

the second tree
— — —

there is not a third —
none where I am
not here

        now — empty
how much emptiness may i consume

it (the emptiness) was not expected
        here —
the whir past my head filled

n
o
t
h
i
n
g

there is one measure

e

          (notice inside the e, there is
nothing)

the sky is blue
it does not exist
still it is blue
the sky is not blue
it is empty

          there is no sky
          a placehold

          it does not exist
          a nonbeing
          a nonexistence —

the sky is blue
the sky is not blue
the sky is there
the sky is not there
where I stand on the pediment
of there
while here
I am here
I am there
I am a pronoun
          measured in emptiness

august nights

only when crickets rub their back legs
will it seem like august
sounding like yet another time
some time ago

when I caught them
put them in a jar, crickets —
with a lid

their back legs like mine run in space
my legs do not make music
burning with desire of sound forgotten
of another animal, a legged animal

between mine wet with noise
a sound of august nights
a noise in wet
not in a jar

glassed in
in a daze making noise
upon august nights

Before I Die

a few minutes, or a few months
or, if lucky, a few years
before i die
i shall wake up

and what will i wonder then?
that i don't wonder now

was it but a dream? fuzzy
details missing
no ending but for now, sketchy

as an abstract charcoal mark
on paper resonating with plant life
from under water it came
reeds read me

read my lines

my sketchy charcoal lines
being rubbed, smeared
into brown edged torn tattered paper
rolled up in a corner
yet

She Sat Beside Herself with a Note
from Him
    after: Gertrude Stein, "there, there"

If you'd been
there yourself/aware of their strangeness
behind the door
there/there was no return/through
that one door/
where she thought/there
was something/
to hold on to

Unfamiliar/as you are now
      in that thing/
      that unmentionable
that "there" of you/
of who you were then

Obvious, now/
Where did you go then?
when asked of you/
there wasn't you/
there
that I could see
or know
from this maybe future
         point

and mine

your absence could never match your
presence
but, when I think of it, you've never been
here or there

not quite there
but here, as not before
then there was "then"

looking in the glass before I drink
there is you there
you are there
without a doubt

why

you are there in my glass
floating on a not volatile
fading cooling surface
such as you are
there

when

i am reminded, no, every moment
you are there in puddles
that i love to stamp and make you wave
like you were there as never before

which brings up the feeling, the question
as never before

you were here badly
somehow your presence
now known — is best without you

The Passing of Me

the passing of me
written on the bottom of clouds
was shorter than I had expected

a few lines
written in prose
some remembered
some saved for the future
lines in Latin
which I could not read
they recited themselves —

"Don't let the bastards wear you down"

Pigeon's Morsel

alongside her feet
pigeon
dismisses her
        wings her on

seated, her orange crepe dress
flutters nearly breathless
over a chair
along a sidewalk

she invites him, a grey cold heartless
pigeon
from rooftops
he darts from a cornice
focuses on one used morsel

alone this pigeon escorts comfort
at the Brasserie Montmartre
outside

he pulls up a faux bamboo chair
"Plastic," he says
with painted lines for the bamboo's nodes
I notice similar marks on his left wing

he flutters, nervous, his tie is crooked
loosened at the neck
collar open
he orders oysters
three for him, three for her

he balks, "it's hot, it's not Paris."
the oysters are warm
his greyness returns
his wings ruffle open
his tie swings
he leaves the table

she swallows
his two abandoned oysters
sliding wet —warm luxury
they land as pigeons' morsels

the men I have not adored

my lips will not find you
my lips are numb where you won't find
me

who will do my thinking
while you're gone
while a bug sits on a leaf eyeing me
for all that I am worth, while
a caterpillar climbs on a leaf
and says —
Wasn't it you —
— Who used to smoke with me

you may be thinking of me
and where
the arc crosses a meridian
with your shallowness —your weakened
self
unaware
in your lost guise —
of whatever ails you

not spoken
—dampened in your voice
which sounds familiar
has been looked upon as strange
as if anyone could be at my door
the address never having been known
never could have been live

you did not belong then, without

a will to do so
to live, to surrender, though
contemplation tried
and failed to see —
is there any fragile truth?
as you
are
not
fragile
through your smoke screen
you turn green
as we speak, illuminated
still standing at the door
while you spin your keys
then fall to your knees, then you think
you can come in

even though there is no one home, not
even the caterpillar who spits in the
house terrarium jungle created by you
with miniature plants with plausible
DNA and butter for sustenance which
I saw you sharing from your fingertip
you lick, they lick, you both smile
between —
your tongue, greedy strange looks
half-closed eyelids, never flutter even
a little

then you close the door, outside is your
boat
nested, your plane nested on your trailer
a life suspended, *coitus interruptus* —
coming here with ID, all being nested

in one another, nested suspended to
a roof top nest

then you close the door without
recollection for the manuscript that
I sent to you, slow on the
uptake, your eyes grew big as the
wheels of your plane, you ran into
the closet to hide —
you were there again
amongst the clothing
and not breathing

just now i am me

due to her recent enlightenment
she has let forth
from deep within the crack in her heart
where the rhymes and the feelings laid
not reluctantly, but with *joie de vivre*
as let free to follow another's far braver
steps

no words of mine can match her bravery
but intent may overlap
as i too have fallen, betrayed, while i
watched it unfold

for all to see she did that
as i could not
as i had so much to hide
did i do that to me
or did he do that to me?
or did he do this to me?

this cannot be i thought smugly
denial of a broken heart is clearly (only
just now)
for the un-denying, the feign of heart
the low, the blinded, the passive
perhaps then that was me
my ugly little ego reared its multiple
headed gargoyles
embrace it now, or be not
it has let me be free
from neglect, from deceit

from looks of malice feigned with love
from the hunched over shoulders that
spoke
of nothing
from the greed
from the seed of non
you are not you
but now you are you
just now I am me
and free to be

profound state of unease

ecology

In Creation

In creation
monkeys have made humans of us

while elephants support without a sigh
step
        by
                slow
                        step

walls and wills filled
        by graying humans
        and their waiting staffs

then their children
waiting
                still
        creating more

Moonlit Leaves
    Sypes Canyon

How the light lies
        on these leaves
while they brushed my neck —
        the moonlit leaves

not on purpose do they

in their moonlit evening
        from a leaf's touch
while I picked
        the moon from the sky
placed it on your forehead

the leaves   jittered
                shaking day
into

        a moon-lit night
from your limbs to my limbs

on my neck where the leaves have
        been
        that touched me and moved me

leaving you

chasing rabbits

leaves jitter
tingling
bugging bugs
in their new greenness
the leaves
when fully in their form
less jiggling
of green
seeds spring emerging, fleeing
sticky with desire
only second to their new greenness

      they dance tingle jitter
touch spring to a catapult
      their stickiness
      in their desire

adhere to something
a greater intention then
previously ever known
intentional joy
while a car chases backwards
catching seeds in its lips
chasing rabbits are we

The Cello Project

*—the cellist drew a bow
      while I drew my breath —*

I envisioned polar bears
I remembered a film
from the thirties
of the shooting of a huge —
b e a u t i f u l
polar bear, who was
skinned, stripped naked bare —
to freeze without its skin —

On its land of snow and ice
at the tundra of bears
fur was for vanity
bears lived in their naked fur
floated on chunks of ice
in a less than brave world

*the starfish tattoo on the cellist's back
moved with her shoulder
while a blue octopus
hung one beautiful tentacle
over her shoulder
and drank from her bare breast —*

The Secret Life of Her

It existed not to her, but to everyone who
knew her:
it was created from her pain
her skin
the way she talked
the way she walked, her sway

The secret life of her
existed in her mind which everyone
could read
"touch me"
then you will have known her

The secret life of her
"i am braille. touch." you can now read
her pain
What does it say?
How can it as it does not have a voice?
and its secrets are heard

The secret life of her
exists as we muse, amuse, *amuse-bouche*
amuse ourselves through our talk of her
which amuses the secret life of her

The secret life of her
wrapped in a blanket
the mule deer's skin, a blanket of hollow
hair, comfort fill
a hyper-extension of its amused voice
bellowing madness of the skin becoming

mouth-blown flesh
the secret life of her

With His Breath

He lays down the poker
as if it were a word
        just behind him
        onto the floor

the fire becomes lit
and there
        he is
        beside himself
        in admiration for fire

that lights him
        already ablaze
with his breath
        he makes words
        using the same breath

ignited
from before he was a man
        at a time when fire
        was not acquainted
        with him
        was not known to him

then
        or to me
        until now

with his breath

Clothes Lines

our lines are so

       that I could follow

sheets of women
silhouettes   against   walls

where —
they
dance in circles
to rejoice in the same place

the women, we —
we bend, we fold
we yield —
to hunger

only then do we

not

leave

Narcissus

49

The flower, the flower
smells upon itself
        love
        at reflective sight
a scent so dear
        as an *intox*
        to deceive, to trick
reminiscent
        of a cloud without shadow
        of a meadow without bees
        a field of words
where Nemesis echoes the scent

upon which
        upon which
we are
        we are
a scent such to become
        a narcissus of ourselves
not fallen, not guilty
and not amongst us

yet dear to one
        by oneself
that lands
                in a pool: hubris
        that ends there

lying in a pool
        of oneself
        a *sfumato*

of air—on water
brushed with—

Lip It

Fat or non-plumped lips, pumped
artificial color that lumps in creases—
Did we ever buy that color?
Was it the name we bought?
My plumped-lips talk paint:

Oh, for sure
Morning-after
Dark waters
Rising peach
Morning bliss
Wet spot
Yo
Not now
Sunrise gloom
I said no
Who said that?
WTF
Circles around you
Go to bed
Nothing is for dinner
Where is my car?
Beard-burn?
Suck on it
Wet spot?
Fish hook?
I didn't hear you
Where are my fucking keys?
Who are you?
You look terrible
I know

You drive
I don't have a clue
What you selling?
You said today
I don't remember you
When was that?
Here's dinner
Was that a rubber?
So, that was it?
Get in the fucking car
Whose keys are these?
Mom's coming
What'd you say your name was?
WTF
I said so
Where are my keys?

Read my painted lips—

sfumato of her lips

ekphrastic

Small Shadows
   A Visit to the Louvre

The small shadows at the corners
of her mouth
move only slightly, recede
without eye contact
without eye movement
or a blink

her small shadows
move
move only slightly
when corners indent
themselves

into:

only she knows
the corners of her mouth
eyelids down, not demure
yet intent

giving way to her mind, she smiles
sees into us with her freedom
her own
her own time

of wonder

the small shadows, a
sfumato of her lips, her mouth
her mind

at the corners of her lips
at the corners of her lovely mouth
lovely they move
without
voice

The Art of Distance

If there is an art to it
it is subtle
abstract or known in silence
as Andy Goldsworthy stone cairns
that are —
or color field paintings of Mark Rothko

the space in between —
undeniably sacred
between you and me
like you in my distance

a distance at the lily pads
strewn across 80 feet of canvas —
the aqueous ponds of Claude Monet
cannot move being caught
in the art of distance, being —
of thought who cannot cross

distance in the art of being
seeing you there
the *Four Seasons* paintings by Kandinsky
where one cannot move being held
while in their presence they hold —

to hear the piano
of Erik Satie with fingers distanced
held in space
of *Gymnopédie No.1*
a nuanced distance between
being and not —

in the art of distance
I surrender to you, I heed you
through and through
the distance between us sacred
real and surreal
to you I surrender — in the distance of me

Paterson's Way

*The romanticism of Paterson's artistic
isolation, of the solitary pursuit of art by a
seeming separate inspiration, is an
intoxicating myth.*
— Richard Brody, Review of the
film, *Paterson* in *The New Yorker*, Dec.
30, 2016

I cannot seem to tear
        myself away
        from the silence

that alone listens to me

like snow
dropping on frozen ground
        with little pings
        a sound I remember

in the silence
        that I choose
footsteps not silenced
through hills and paths
in the silence I hear it all

I cannot seem to tear
        myself away
        from the silence
I listen to nothing
        yet hear it all
not kept under wraps
        of cloth woven

          loom to loom
some other time
from great silence
I cannot seem to tear
          myself away
          from the quiet
deliberate of word
          room to room
deliberate of silence
          and if in the rain
one can tell another
on one side that beckons
rejects
          one
that mis-fits
          one
beguiles
          one
misleads
          one
into a land or a place
opted by a bus
to a place without stops
this journey of silence
through a gear
          a shift
          a grind
          heave to the haul
my road needs no map
awakens to the people there
          with face
          with value
          disrobed
          no address

the only thing they know
        is now
        the silence of us
where there are no stops
        or whistles
air puffs open the doors
        to clinging silence
        sucks one out the door
to a street of bricks
        and cats
        without preference
to alleys or sidewalks
        only here
on this brick or two
to own a place without stops
of a bus going by
with a lung of desire
breathed into itself
        at the next stop
where the twins lived
one at the front door
one at the rear door
        of their street

morning of silence
        precious
appears at all
        gradually
letting go of night
letting go of desire
        since the day before
written as words appeared overhead
        a voice over
        says my lines

that allude to risk
          to candor
          I won't let go
          of this day
where you were just then
in the dawn of my content
          soft, yielding

I cannot seem to tear
          myself away
          from the silence
compelling my silence
not prodding
          being there
          with
          admittance
the light of being
hears my silence
when the lungs puff open
          the doors
at your stop
where then I can begin again

Alice and Me

1
Alice followed me with a skip
she pointed a finger —
to the plane that lunged from above —
the Mad Hatter at the controls
the woods and the ferns
and shrooms taken
from there

2
While not the Houses of Parliament —
torn from woeful sad bridges
where we, Alice and I, scrawled with
lipstick
I Love You All
Alice followed from the museum
to be here by my side of curiosity
as we squeezed down into the hole
before the bomb hit the towers
with sinew and bones with diamonds

3
With you, you creepy Dodo —
you couldn't make it through
another year
devouring those deplorable worms —
pseudo lamentations, sitting
on a shore watching wave
after wave with that
dumb look foretelling
a future of bond salesmen —

and aqueducts —
and Cadillacs —
little licks from the moon

4
Alice tasted the fenugreek
of yesterday in the pot boiling
madly with tea cakes —
and little bombs

Biutiful
     a film by Alejandro Gonzales
     Iñárritu

shake my soul to run
thru pastoral rain soaked fields
some with nonchalance

the chance meeting
where the father within her
could not escape his whims

danced on the fire escape
while a box of tomatoes wilted
had gone over—
          —over the edge of desire

umbrella—scrawny, threadbare—
ribbed skeleton let the rain through—
drenched one, whose desire was
matchless:
she held nothing against him
she desired nothing
less than herself—

My Own Cave

"So close to civilization is the cave."
Roger Ebert in reference to Luis Buñuel
film: *The Exterminating Angel*

To exterminate is to harm that I do not
want
you shall not go with me into that
darkened corner
where we find ourselves still
where we'd have come out the cave

a warm touchable quiet
harbored you there in my cave
when we painted on the walls
our hands splayed, savored over them
touched each ridge, each valley
with our finger tips
spread wide with a reed as a spray
outlined our fingers with the juice of
berries

I was here in my cave so far
from civilization—so far from the light
of anything that would show the way—
the way out where I stay

quiet in solitude

IN DUCTION
  Concerning the Spiritual in Art
  Vassily Kandinsky

        art is   child

        and   mother

art

                never   repeated

~~past~~   produce   ~~still~~
~~born~~
live

                          strive

          Greek   ~~methods~~

                   similar

form   soulless

                      aping monkey

resembles   ~~human~~   ~~he~~

~~will~~

sit

                                  actions

        no ~~real~~ meaning

external ~~similarity~~

founded   ~~fundamental~~ truth

inner tendency

moral   spiritual

~~ideals~~

lost

inner

feeling

external forms

express   inner feelings

earlier   sympathy

spiritual

Primitives

artists

express

~~internal~~ truths   renounce

~~external~~

form

The Refusal of Time
    William Kentridge
    Refusal of Time
    Museum of Modern Art, 2017
    San Francisco, CA

Time
an operatic voiceover opens
with French horns and trumpets
bath tubs roll by
        as
        drums

people, women, children
        dance
perpetual wooden machines
        with a low hum of moving parts
        swish by
        whispers working

a refusal of time
a march of humanity
butterflies flights magnetized
        become pictures
then fall again
        pieces of butterflies
        disappear time again

relentless kinetic power
        humans march
        to the refusal

of time
incessant

all time is past time

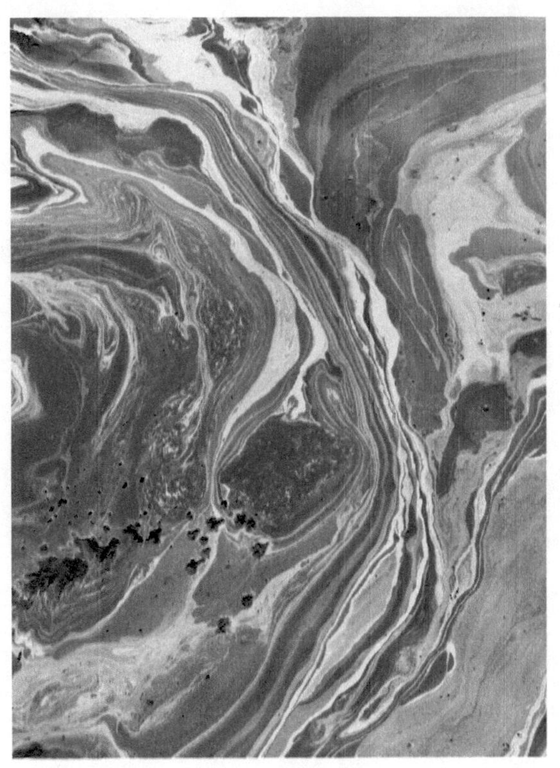

entwined vines

love

I Have Loved You

Had I but known how to love you
with your tendrils of vine
        tender in a dark place
        displaced particle after particle
        deep into a surface
twisting stems that need you
        need us to want you

take them to the stream's edge
tendrils bring leaves
        you there
where I have loved you before the sand
        the dirt
        the rain

as a scented leaf fell
as I see you there now before me
with leaf's stem dangling from your teeth

where the spring sighs

the last time I drank of the spring
you spoke in waves
with their movement through your hair

the words were smeared
blurry as graffiti
like lips
lacking all but intention

hearing less then I realized
how could I have shared the house
on the South meadow
where the spring sighs

with you gone

My Alice

Alice followed me with a skip
and pointed a finger
not to just anywhere
not to here my dear

But above to the plane
that spun with the Mad Hatter
at the controls
above the wood, ferns and shrooms
and not the Houses of Parliament
or their woefully sad bridges

Where Alice and I wrote on the walls
with lipstick
in a royal color

I love you all
Alice followed me from the museum
then down we went into the hole

Entwined Vines

They touched them where
the linger of your memory
defied itself:
dizzy while with gravity—

My gypsy came near
the littoral of the cove
where we had to climb
on our bellies
through—
dampened sea moss
kelp and entwined vines

Epiphytic flowers bloomed—
hung over our eyes—
gazed back at us
did not see anything
but love

The Moon and You

To what do we owe
        the taste of the moon?
your silence comes
to mind —
your decadence
of doing nothing
that I or anyone can see
        as progress
of anything
while the moon sees it all

gently, only in moonlight
when turned the other way
you are nothing
        but a shadow
of your former self

best left undone
you know nothing of
the moon

edges

when I took my edge off
there was nothing inside
realizing what the edge held
together was nothing:
          glands, sinew, cells, a heart

no memory held
a thought
while the mind went everywhere
of its own accord
with the edges removed

Flower Petals

petals
along the way
set free to the wind

languishing little

pollen laid along curbs
surrendered destiny
for the moment only he
holds her destiny
not to be free again
to any one

feeling his moist lips
accepting only
      flower petals from his lips
come to her lips
reading
his lines in the petals

His Hair Like Wings

His hair like wings
His hair blows
to the sides flying
    held by a found sailor cap
gold cord came later
    (if ever)

His shoulders hang a coat
nine hundred sixty-five threads worsted
yet threadbare

His hair takes flight
off he lifts
newspaper in teeth
carrying a rose hip bough
one green berry clings
one red is going
a bell rings: cha ching

    Sirens sing

He falls to earth, into the river
he swims to a forgotten shore
applause beckons him
where trumpeters sing
white in feathered wings
at his awaiting shore

still the Sirens sing
    Welcome

my memories

i drank my memory down
to place less defined than felt
drinking absinthe as disguise
thickened by time
a fairy light expression
muddled with you in the glass
hours and minutes, even
months and   years —

lying at the bottom of the glass
        green liquid —

on the rim stands a father
diving headlong into the English people
poking flowers, wormwood and fennel
bringing with him straw and words
that bedded her in bubbles and squeak
squeaking out children, curtailed by
blurred   vision —
hardly divine

Wings My Whisper
    Siltcoos Lake

If I stay here long
I shall speak in a whisper
if I lived here in the wood
        I would not speak

The sound, a rush, a flock
        as they fly parallel
over the lake's obsidian waters
        glasslike, blackish-green
wings dip into the water
        with a flash
        they spray

Winging it as they do
        sloshing waves with their wings
        bathing their feathered backs
bathing in sounds   parallel

Siltcoos Lake
        obsidian in nature
        thrown here
        shiny there

Shiny, it springs
an echo under my whisper
the sound, a rush
        by flock
        they are my only music

/Us in a Timezone

our eyelids have little in common
blinking in disbelief/then closing
like a sunning butterfly
they/not in disbelief
winged together as our eyelids
        wing one another on
in place/in this timezone
man made/
subjective timezones

are we in our demise, our found-ness
in any time/now?
a place unknown to bees/ants/and
stinging nettles

ponds mirror me/but I see you
there/while in another timezone/where
on a sophisticated lake/acquiescent
quicker than we knew
would come back to us
stinging nettles burn long in
remembrance
        on one's skin
not like rosemary
fondly/but stringent
remember me says the want—
the desire

you might drive up to my open door
find me there/
not with trivets or Boxwood—

painted fences
but pine/Vine Maple and Lupine
waiting to bloom in wildness
leading the way to a door
you see us/I see me
in a different timezone

in memory: the air

nature/eco-nature

Elegy for a Douglas Fir

            Drawn into my eyes
                                        the
way the flat needles
            hold glamour
                                    until the tip
lets fall a drip
            circles back for more
                                        with
richness imbued
                gives nurture and
sustenance

            slugs in its duff
            creatures rooted
                    maggots, worms, spiraling
centipedes
                        uprooted

                                I stand by
that tree
            coming down after eighty years

limb by limb by limb
                    top off—then the mid off
                        branches lopped
                                            tree
killer swings
            in my tree
                                sings a
sotto voce lament
            I want to feel this tree

                                        as
hummingbirds suspend
          ants scatter

while I watch:
              which one are you?

watcher?
               killer?
        stalker?
                            whose eyes could
rest there —

distracted —
                                  transfixed —
         wide spaces in its gnarled bark

nearly sag to a frown
          as the arborist
                            sings the
Magic Flute
                  it leaves no take, limb by
limb

it produces nothing

              so much
        as this —

Coastal Range

My being in the coastal range
        disregards
a global position —

invisible as I am here
        the coast, the sea
        the end —
—the beginning
        of us —

skeletal lichens hang
        on branches
        soak up memory
        toxins —
        things that may never have

happened —
        until now
—without us —

Hummingbirds

8.14 am
        An early morning
train blows through
        tyrant like
blinding my hummingbirds
sugar water feeder
makes puddles on the
        patio below —
to feed the ants

the sun drinks through
glass in early — morning
        birds reflect
their absence

9.23 am
        I sit in a breeze
a ruffle of leaves
a bird has come
        to my side
        looks to see if I am
edible — &
my head in mirrored-ness
analytical within its bird head
        my hummingbird — comes
to my prepared

elixir that drips below

9.46 am
        the calm ruffle of leaves
leaves the air warm while I covet
        my angst —
drifts & fades
into the sun's shadows

the hummingbird
        sits subsumed
then a fluorescent flash
a flash of magenta
a rapid green whir
        & disappears

Limb by Limb

bark holds you in
where you harbor years
rings of weather and fire

your flesh—
craggy with insects and moss

my arms climb
my limb to your limb
limb by limb by limb
to where the moss drapes
in acquiescent light
succulent as a bed
the color takes me in
the moss feeds me

I want your limbs to want me
I am within your reach

The Spring

Within a meadow flanked by service
berries and yews
with sixty foot Douglas Firs
whose branches touch to sweep the
	ground
sway and tremble with the slightest wind
with a load of snow or a single bird

friends pick blossoms to make flower
	crowns
grown along the edge of meadow grasses
one by one flower stems weave together

a woman carries a vessel
with the precious spring water
hidden deeper in the wood
with instructions from her lover —
long since gone, on how to carry the
	vessel
to carry water from the spring

the grasses were tall
filled with thistle, beetle, and bottle
a path seen below the roots
with barefoot tracks
written into soil that led from the spring

Sandy River

                    A river of sandy
bottoms —
the color pure

from spring melt
     swollen with silt and ash
                       mineral and
     dust
as a celadon vessel —

     lying
          horizontal —
                  —a
vase
turned its own way
     to contain the waters

—its land parts
an eddy swirls
            — a celadon vessel
lies
between
        two banks
                —a
meander
to another river
          to lie upon

Andaman Sea

A child's hands catch drips
as he leans forward
        as if in penance
receives a sacred stream

off a sheet of gray tin
        from the awning above
his mother's shop

his toes curl over the curb
with cabbage and plastic bags

Buddhist ceremonial icons
        all gold and silver
encircle trees with marigolds

when years later he would lean
        his shaved head
        from under a different awning
on an island
in the Andaman Sea

he sees his mother
smile at him in his palms
        that hold
        his water to drink

Nature Retreat

Fold upon fold the light creeps
its way towards dark
it can rest there
where it may begin to feel —
begin to see less
of the folds
of steps going
to take us nowhere

of necessity I have learned to like
          even love
a path I hope not to regret
my love as well —

one fumbling step will see us down
a child's hand carries bamboo stalks
to help others up the steps
as we go not to our last

remembering the deep
deities have a hold on water
if you can hold it in your hands
that still you
          beckon you to a door
          it will be there

there is not a door, only a way
          orchids
          do not wilt as I have

where it then goes dark
suddenly lovely—

Light Beyond the Trees

watching the light change at the end of
trees
scrambled silhouette in milky pre-dawn
imagined by the lingering setting moon

a soft warm breath whispered damp
feathers
along my cheek, pernicious night —
cheeks sunk into creeks of watery reeds

seeing soul after soul in the stream
blades of grass as bed
dewy as swaddled flannel sheets

that floated along a stream of night
enveloped thinly in footed bed
inarticulate and thin while warm

awakened by precious light
beyond the trees — moving into day
ended my long lonely night

the brush with wings of milky intent
that nearly swept me away
into sublimity —

ode to green

green
how delicious on my leaf you look
along with sun you become lime
a green you do to me
translucent green —

how many shades
can become sweet
how delicious is green
on my leaf you lie
warm, not un-tender
as strong my leaf of green —

green and delicious, I am leaf
to you

anguish that i held

emotion

anguish

the anguish that I held so dear
beside me for its use
of misused, misbegotten
badly arranged and harebrained
as a place to harbor in the cupboard

the goods ran out along with a man
a cupboard still hangs on a wall
my anguish followed him out the door
baring studs in the wall
by a nail it hangs

little remains that has not slid away

having followed him there
the anguish at the door
that never fit
never quite closed
the flood, the snow, the cold

I existed full of anguish
as ill-conceived, as absolute
my constant state of fear
for reasons unknown

bestowed on me?
to be so full of despair
where is it now?
not an emptiness, but filled

with the misery, the confusion
an anguish that was

Fog at the Door

upon waking
from over there
while here
opening eyes to a surprise
the ceiling of a life
      unfamiliar

"where did the glitter come from?"

the run on the floor
hosting the door
      guarding —
came from over there
that couldn't have belonged

beyond the door
nothing —
      grayness
hosting a fog
as one would suspect
stays on the chair

is not there —
the chair, without a seat
for anyone
      now alone with her fog
has ever sat there
      grayness like fog

through her door
in her annexed room

beyond the door
lists
paper words in columns
decrying nothing of fog
beyond the door
in comes the tripping fog
of another color
        at her door

The Seagull and the River

a fog lies on the river
with imbued grayness
the Columbia gives way
        to sky
        —melting
with sky drinking sky
        fog devours the river

foundling seagull
denied her flight
        with only one wing
having been disarmed
        her other wing waved
        with a left wing yield

thirty-nine degree river
        ashen shards float
        denied frozenness
unarmed she went to sea
wearing her left wing
smiling she swam in circles
        a tribal dance, yet singular
        her own dance

        cunning river drank the sky
        tasting grayness
river sheltered with sky
it drank of itself
        wet
        cold
and not denied

Moonlight as Snow

when snow   lies
on tree branches
      spilling to the deck below

through a window
as still can be
over the   sill
puddling and whitening

brings a presence
      awakens
        yet eyes   sleep

the light it spreads
flattens
               spills
loud from the humors
of the moon

               still
in its knowledge
its multilingual
presence
               awakens
     anoints our minds
the light is spread
              flattens

and sparkles
has
              flow

just now snow on the sill
and below

the poker and the fire

he lays down the poker
as if it were a word
onto the floor
        just behind him

the fire has become lit
and he is beside himself
in admiration for fire
        that lights the sky

with his breath, that makes words
with the same breath
that makes fire
        ignites him

before he was a man
at a time before fire
        acquainted man

she had not known him
        as fire
        before now

Wave

the wave curls—
uncurls
stands like a glass pane
stretched, flattened

bluest shine—taunt it stretches—
hangs—
stands suspended there

we lie upon the sand
together spent and wet
we watch a wave stand, curl—
recoil, crash
feelings for one another
near breathless
like waves ourselves
particles suspend upon
themselves

roaming to swim freely
relentless in that arc
arcing into one self
perfectly chaotic
physics undone, unknown
particular matter
suspended long enough
suspended in standing animation

before the curl—stretch, stand, curl, fall

this presence—collapses

un-curls, hurls
somehow becomes wave again
to be swept away
again

Existence

what am i now —
—i ask
and i cannot answer
we are all made, just plain made
no reason, but this:

existence, only once may we exist

there is no answer
that can exist now
we are all —

out of love or lust

possibly intention —
making a person
has that ever been
conscious —

"think I forgot how to be happy"
is still my existential
question

i was made for this —

About the Author

Diane Corson claims that poems and words float on rivers, on waves, hang in trees. She was a featured poet at an event for the Portland Transit System and she has served on the executive board of the Oregon Poetry Association.

Diane Corson's poetry is in the collection of Oregon Poetry at the University of Oregon Library. She has been published in the 2003 *Poetry Anthology, Theory Magazine, Terratory Journal,* the *North Coast Squid, Cirque Journal,* 2017, *Cirque Journal,* 2018, *Terra Incognito, Pif Magazine,* 2020, and *pān đé mïk, an Anthology of Pandemic Poems.* She was also the featured artist and poet for the 2022 Edition of *Triggerfish Critical Review.*

Diane Corson has written and designed
three chapbooks: *Poor Tree*, 2014,
elemental, 2016, and *There Being: Interiority*,
2018. She has an art and design degree
from Montana State University in
Bozeman, Montana, where she lived a
fairly primitive life for thirty years before
moving to the Pacific Northwest.

About the Book

Lucy Cotter, PhD

Like a contemporary Emily Dickinson, Diane Corson hones in on the minutiae of everyday life as a portal to the interdependence of human and nonhuman beings. She is at her most starkly original in deconstructed poems like *empty emptiness*, which belie her entry point into language from visual art, unencumbered by academic syntax and linear thinking…

Often multi-directional and seeping into other realms through meditations on form or color, Corson re-enchants the banal, yet carries an ecofeminist undertone that gently invokes the precariousness of our current moment. Her poetic bandwidth is wide, encompassing contemplations on the natural world (*Sandy River, Elegy for a Douglas Fir*), an embrace of the imperfect pleasures of love (*the men I have not adored, With His Breath*), and occasional speculative escapades (*Alice and Me, How I Made It*). Corson's singularity of vision lies in her infectious fascination with the permeable boundaries of self in the world.

Tristan Beach, MFA

Diane Corson's poems are painterly and visually precise, unveiling through their experimental lyrical structures the minutia of relationships within the self and the world. The poet's self of each poem is stretched and split, disseminated across ancient ceremony (*The Spring*), spatiotemporal distance (*/Us in a Timezone*), print text (*IN DUCTION*), and watery forms (*Wave, Coastal Range, The Seagull and the River*). The poet's intimate noticing of the world displays the animacy of living and non-living beings through brief, wending lines that call into question the very idea of separateness (*Fog at the Door*). While these poems run from the erotic *(I have Loved You)* to the political ("To exterminate is to harm that I do not want," *My Own Cave*), they share a vocabulary of things: paintings, ants, hummingbirds, tendrils, the moon, lips, the sea. Common among these poems is Corson's fascination with familiar life, in which kinship emerges through acts, objects, and memory: "sheets of women / silhouettes   against   walls /… / the women, we — / we bend, we fold" (*Clothes Lines*). Ultimately, Corson's poems converse with one another, inviting the reader into quiet, inquisitive moments of relation.

Colophon

The text of *Along the Fault of Me* is set in Cochin which is a serif typeface. It was originally produced in 1912 by Georges Peignot of the Paris foundry G. Peignot et Fils (future Deberny and Peignot) and was based on the copperplate engravings of 18th century French artist Charles-Nicholas Cochin, from which the typeface takes its name.

Paper: Uncoated 50 lb Crème
Book design:
      Diane Corson
      B Sedgwick
      Portland, Oregon
Produced through Ingram Spark
      Worldwide